WALT DISNEY PICTURES presents
WARREN BEATTY
DICK TRACY
Music by DANNY ELFMAN
Co-Producer JON LANDAU
Editor RICHARD MARKS
Production Designer RICHARD SYLBERT
Cinematography by VITTORIO STORARO, A.I.C.-A.S.C.
Executive Producers BARRIE M. OSBORNE
and ART LINSON & FLOYD MUTRUX
Written by JIM CASH & JACK EPPS, JR.
Produced and Directed by WARREN BEATTY
"Dick Tracy" Album Available On Sire Records
Produced in association with
SILVER SCREEN PARTNERS IV
Dolby Stereo® Selected Theatres
Distributed by Buena Vista Pictures Distribution, Inc.
© 1990 THE WALT DISNEY COMPANY
Novelization by A. L. SINGER

A GOLDEN BOOK • NEW YORK
Western Publishing Company, Inc., Racine, Wisconsin 53404

© 1990 The Walt Disney Company. All rights reserved. Printed in the U.S.A. No part of this book may be reproduced or copied in any form without written permission from the copyright owner. GOLDEN, GOLDEN & DESIGN, GOLDENCRAFT, and A GOLDEN BOOK are trademarks of Western Publishing Company, Inc. Library of Congress Catalog Card Number: 90-81683
ISBN: 0-307-12401-0   A B C D E F G H I J K L M

The kid ducked into an old garage. He crouched in the doorway and peeked out. He was in luck. The cops walked by, never noticing him. He sighed with relief. It was tough being on the run all the time, but anything—even living in the streets—was better than being sent to that orphanage again.

Just then he heard the roar of an engine behind him, then a crash. He dived back into the shadows when he heard the blasting of a tommy gun.

It was over as quickly as it began. When he slowly stood up, he saw what had happened.

He saw the five tough guys who had been gunned down in the middle of a card game. He saw the car that had crashed through the door, and the man with the flat-topped skull who was holding the tommy gun. The kid turned to run. With a loud clang, his foot hit a trash can. Looking over his shoulder in fear, he realized that he'd been seen.

The gunman whirled around and took aim.

The kid had never run so fast in his life.

The gunman fired his tommy gun at the wall, tracing out a message in charred bullet holes:

EAT LEAD TRACY

"Calling Dick Tracy...Calling Dick Tracy...We've got five dead men at the Seventh Street Garage, and nobody knows who they are," Officer Pat Patton called into his wrist-radio. *"You'd better get over here right away."*

When the message crackled over Dick Tracy's wrist-radio, he was at an opera. His girlfriend, Tess Trueheart, rolled her eyes. Their date was over.

"I'll be back," Tracy said. He raced to the garage. Pat was there, along with Officer Sam Catchem and Police Chief Jim Brandon. None of them had seen anything like this. Five deaths, no IDs, no clues. They knew there was only one man who could figure this out—the man whose name was carved into the wall with bullet holes.

They were right. Detective Dick Tracy never forgot a face. It was his job. "These guys all worked for Lips Manlis," he said.

"So who's out to get Lips?" Sam asked.

"Big Boy Caprice," Tracy replied. "And the next time, his boys will be writing our names on our *backs.*"

Pat and Sam fell silent. They read Tracy's message loud and clear. There was a war on, a war to control the streets. Anyone in Big Boy's way had better watch out, including the cops.

To follow Tracy, turn to page 22.
Where's the kid? Find out on page 19.

Tracy and the Kid bolted for the stairs. The entire room shook as they climbed to the top and ran out of the building.

With the force of a bomb, the furnace exploded.

Tracy and the Kid were knocked off their feet. They landed on the sidewalk, bruised but alive.

As the smoke cleared, a disapproving look came over the Kid's face. "Gee, Tracy, that was a lot of dough!"

Tracy gave him a smile. "You're all right, Kid."

Standing in his office with Tess, Chief Brandon, and the Kid, Tracy felt frustrated. He had gone home after the explosion to find his wallet and badge missing. But his mood was picking up. He listened as Brandon read from a scroll: " 'For action in the face of grave danger, the Kid'—whose name will be filled in later when he picks one out—'is awarded this Honorary Detective Certificate and badge.' "

The Kid beamed happily as Tracy pinned a badge on his shirt. "Tracy," he whispered, "I got a badge for *you*." He glanced at Tracy's desk. "In the top drawer."

"What?" Tracy opened the drawer to find his badge pinned to his wallet. He broke into a smile and stuck out his hand to the Kid. "Put 'er there, Detective!"

Across the room, Brandon pulled Tess aside. "What about the orphanage?" he muttered.

"We put it off till tomorrow," Tess said.

That afternoon Tracy was called to City Hall, where D.A. Fletcher gave him another warning about Big Boy.

"Are you telling me not to pull Caprice in?" Tracy asked in disbelief.

"You've done it five times, and he's never been convicted," Fletcher replied. "Besides, fourteen witnesses insist he spent the entire morning at a dance lesson. I'm sorry."

Tracy stood there, stunned, as Fletcher walked off.

That night, standing in a dark, chilly cemetery, Big Boy frowned as he listened to complaints from the gentleman beside him.

When Big Boy had heard enough, he said, "What's the matter, we're not paying you enough money? Don't tell me about my boys messing up the Tracy rubout. They flunked their test. Now they're flunkies—like you. I don't care if Tracy catches on. It doesn't matter. You're still working for me. When you are dead, *then* you are out. Until then, you are mine. I own you. You are gonna be mayor of my city."

A Catch-a-Crook Adventure

As Big Boy returned to his limousine, D.A. Fletcher's face turned a ghostly shade of white.

Across town, in Tracy's apartment, Breathless was making a surprise visit. No big deal, she was saying. She just wanted to get to know him. But Tracy had one thing on his mind. As long as she was there, he'd try to get her to testify.

She turned to him with a pout. "But if I testify against Big Boy, he'll have me bumped off."

"He'd have to get me first," Tracy said. "I'd be protecting you twenty-four hours a day. That's my job."

Breathless walked toward him, a smile spreading across her face. She wrapped her arms around him and gave him a long, slow kiss. Neither she nor Tracy saw Tess appear at the open door, then move away silently.

Moments later Tracy did hear footsteps clattering in the hallway. He pulled away from Breathless, grabbing a handkerchief to wipe the lipstick off his lips.

When Tess reappeared at the door, she tried to act like she didn't care about what she had seen. Beside her, the Kid almost dropped his ice-cream cone.

"Uh, Tess," Tracy said quickly, "this is—"

"I know," Tess snapped. "Hello, Miss Mahoney."

"You must be Miss Trueheart," Breathless said. "Tracy's told me so much about you." She turned to leave, adding, "We'll be in touch, Tracy."

As Tess stuck a melting ice-cream cone in Tracy's hand, the Kid ran to the window. Watching Breathless leave the building, he said, "Now, *that's* what I call a dame!"

To discover the new plot against Tracy, turn to page 33.
To see opening night at the Club Ritz, turn to page 37.

Breathless Mahoney sang into the mike, looking out over the crowd at the Club Ritz. Most of the men just kept on gambling, but a lot of them smiled back at the gorgeous singer. To them, she was irresistible.

At a table near the stage, Lips Manlis grinned. He had it made. He was one of the City's top crime bosses and he owned the Club Ritz, where gangsters could cheat and gamble in peace.

But the peace was broken when the front door flew open. "Raid! It's the cops!" someone shouted.

Lips turned around calmly while everyone else panicked. As three cops approached, he just smiled.

"You're under arrest," one of them said, "for owning and operating a gambling establishment."

They hustled him and Breathless out through the front door and into a car.

Lips knew he was in trouble when he saw a familiar man in the backseat. The man had a flattened skull, and he was holding a tommy gun.

"Flattop!" Lips exclaimed. He turned to Breathless. "These guys ain't cops!"

"Hiya, Lips" was all Flattop said.

Lips was afraid of only one thing in life—Big Boy Caprice and his gang. Flattop was one of the gang. The other members were waiting at the Southside Warehouse: Numbers, Itchy, Mumbles, and Big Boy himself.

As the car pulled into the warehouse Lips tried to make a run for it. He went two steps before tripping.

Big Boy held out a sheet of paper. "Sign this contract turning the Club Ritz over to me." Watching Lips nervously write his name, Big Boy cracked a walnut in his white-gloved hands. He stuffed the shells into his pocket and ate the rest. "You're dirty, Lips," he said, chewing thoughtfully. "You need a bath."

With a clatter, the sides of a wooden crate snapped up, surrounding Lips. His eyes flashed with fear.

Big Boy gave a signal, and a cement mixer started backing toward the crate.

"Not the bath!" Lips shouted.

But it was too late. The mixer slowly covered him with cement. When the deed was done and the crate was covered, a trapdoor opened below it.

Lips Manlis went plunging into the dark river.

"Put the word out," Big Boy commanded. "Lips's territory is mine now. Everybody who worked for him works for me. Everything he owned, I own. This is my town."

With a chuckle, Big Boy took out another walnut. It was going to be easier than he thought.

Where is Dick Tracy? Turn to page 29.

"*Gambling?*" Big Boy said, looking shocked. "You mean you thought we had *gambling* here?"

Pruneface shook his head. "I wouldn't be caught dead in a place that permitted gambling."

Tracy looked right and left. Out of the corner of his eye he saw the waiter who had disappeared up the stairs moments before. Tracy easily recognized Pat despite the gray wig and waiter's uniform. He also recognized Pat's secret signal. It was time to go. "I'll be back, Big Boy," he said.

"Listen," Big Boy replied, "tell me when you're coming and I'll have a big party."

Tracy turned to leave. "Let's go," he said to the other cops.

Big Boy's brow knitted with suspicion as he turned to Pruneface. "You notice he didn't really look around…"

Outside, Pat ran from the club and jumped into Tracy's car. "They did it!" he said. "Bug and Sam planted the mike, then Sam escaped through the roof."

As they drove into the night Tracy kept his ear to his wrist-radio. Bug Bailey was reliable. When Bug planted a listening device, no one detected it. Now Bug was in the Club's attic, tuned to the conference room below. If all went well, Tracy and his men would be having a busy night.

It took ten minutes for the first message to come in. *"Tracy, this is Bug. They're going to the Acme Diner!"*

The race was on. When Big Boy's men showed up to collect money at the Acme Diner, Tracy was there. When Ribs Mocca held up a market, Tracy was waiting. From the Swank Steakhouse to Pete's Laundry, wherever Big Boy's men showed up Tracy caught them.

The sun still hadn't risen when Big Boy read the newspapers in the Club Ritz conference room. The headlines stared him in the face:

TRACY BATTLES MOB!

CAPRICE EMPIRE CRUMBLES!

Big Boy slammed his fist on the table. "Everywhere I turn, it's Tracy, Tracy, Tracy! It's like he's reading my mind!" He picked up a newspaper and scanned the lead article. "He got Texie Garcia, Ribs Mocca, and Johnny Ramm. Now DeSanto. Who's next?"

"You said you had a way of taking care of Tracy," Pruneface complained. " 'Leave it to me,' you said. Well, let me tell you something. I'm gonna get him myself!"

"You shoot Tracy, they point the finger at me," Big Boy retorted.

In the dark, cramped attic room above them, Bug adjusted the sound level on his equipment. He reached out to grab his coffee when he saw a cockroach crawl into his sandwich.

He swatted at it and the roach skittered away. Bug turned back to his work, furiously taking notes on Big Boy's conversation.

He never noticed that his hand had knocked against his coffee cup and tipped it over.

But downstairs in the conference room, Big Boy noticed when a drop of liquid landed on his newspaper. He tasted it, then looked up at the brown stain that was growing on the ceiling.

Quickly he climbed onto the table and looked into the light fixture.

Big Boy saw the mike hanging there, recording his every word. He began to turn red with anger. Gritting his teeth, he drew his gun.

To find out how Big Boy gets revenge on Bug, turn to page 45.

To find out how Big Boy gets revenge on Tracy, turn to page 55.

Tracy pulled Tess into the doorway. With a *rat-ta-ta-ta-ta-ta-ta-tat*, bullets flew around them. Windows shattered and the pieces crashed to the ground. Garbage cans were sliced in half.

Then, suddenly, the car was gone. Tess breathed a sigh of relief. They were safe.

Tracy ran out to his car. The Kid had been in there the whole time! Was he...?

The Kid answered his question by climbing out of the car. "Let's go get 'em! What're we waiting for?" he shouted.

Those were Tracy's feelings exactly. But he still had some unfinished business—with Tess. He turned to her, wanting to say so much, wanting to talk about their future. But now was the wrong time. He had to go.

"I'm sorry," he said softly.

"Don't be," Tess replied. "When you play in the street, it's part of the game. I know that." She smiled faintly. "Just don't expect me to like it."

Tess sighed as Tracy drove off with the Kid. Tracy had saved her life, but somehow she still felt wounded.

After chasing the car in vain, Tracy and the Kid ended up in Tracy's office. While the detective made some phone calls the Kid fell asleep. Tracy had just begun searching for the getaway car

A Catch-a-Crook Adventure

among police photos when the door opened.

It was Breathless, carrying a long mink stole. As usual, she looked gorgeous.

"I'm so glad you called," she said, sitting on his desk. She smiled at him and leaned closer.

Tracy knew she was trying to be romantic, but he had asked her there for another reason. He located the sapphire earring he'd found in the warehouse. Dangling it in front of her, he said, "I called you here because I want to know if you're ready to testify."

Breathless backed away, looking hurt and sad. "You're right. Why would you want to get mixed up with someone like me? I'll be lucky if I get through the week alive. They probably followed me here." She got up from the desk. "If you want to throw me in jail, go ahead."

Tossing the stole over her shoulder, she left.

Moments later Tracy flew out of his office, pulling his coat around him. He called out to Sam, "Watch the Kid, OK? I want to see where Breathless is going."

To follow Breathless, turn to page 46.
To find out what Big Boy and his men are up to, turn to page 51.

"You OK, Tracy?" Pat called down into the attic.

"Just fine," Tracy replied, looking around. He found a storage barrel and rolled it under the skylight. Then he lugged a heavy table over, rested it on the barrel like a seesaw, and stood on the lower end. "OK, Pat," he called. "Jump!"

Pat leapt through the open skylight. As he fell onto the high end of the table, Tracy was catapulted upward. He flew onto the roof and planted his feet. From where he was standing, he could see Brandon's men gathered outside the club.

Tracy hopped from roof to roof, then slid down a fire escape and ran up to Brandon. "Hiya, Chief!" he called out, grabbing a tommy gun from Sam.

The chief's eyes flashed with amazement at Tracy's stunt.

Tracy looked at the club. He could hear Breathless singing inside. The club's garage doors were bolted shut.

"Chief, Big Boy's got Tess. Bring your men—" Tracy began.

A bone-jarring crash cut him off. The garage doors splintered open as the first car burst through.

The cops dived behind their cars. Tracy took aim with his tommy gun, cutting open the side of the car. It swerved into a fire hydrant, sending water shooting into the air.

A Catch-a-Crook Adventure

When the next car barreled into the street, Tracy shot out a front tire. The car hopped over onto its hood, smashed into a building, and burst into flames.

The third car didn't even make it to the middle of the street. It went out of control, careening over the sidewalk and into Chief Brandon's car. The front door popped open, and out stepped Flattop.

"Give up, Flattop!" Tracy yelled from across the street.

Flattop gritted his teeth. He pointed his tommy gun at Tracy and fired.

Tracy hopped away as the shots whistled past him, then he fired back. Flattop collapsed on the ground in agony.

As fast as it had started, the war was over. The only sound on the street was the gushing of the broken hydrant.

Tess and Big Boy were nowhere to be seen.

Tracy scrambled into the club. The gambling tables were all there; patrons were huddled behind them. Only Breathless seemed unshaken. She sat at the bar, looking over her shoulder at Tracy.

"Where are they?" he demanded.

Breathless pointed to a room behind the piano. "He took her through there. The wine room."

Tracy ran toward the room, but when Breathless called his name, he turned.

Their eyes met for a split second. In the distance Tracy could hear a muffled hooting noise.

With a weak smile Breathless said, "Good luck."

"Thanks," Tracy replied. He ran into the wine room. Immediately his eye caught the strange slant of the opposite wall.

It was a trick wall. He tried pushing it open, but it had been jammed shut.

Boooooooop. That noise again. It sounded like a foghorn. But where could it be coming from? There were no windows in the room, and the foghorn was over by the waterfront. How could the sound reach all the way to the club...?

Suddenly Tracy bolted for the front door. He knew *exactly* where to go, and he couldn't believe how long it had taken him to figure it out.

To find out where Tracy is going, turn to page 25.
To find out where Tess and Big Boy are, turn to page 59.

The kid was running so fast, his feet barely touched the ground. The sunset's glow cast a long, purplish shadow behind him. It wasn't until he was halfway across town that he finally stopped.

As he collapsed onto the stoop of a nearby building, he thought his lungs would explode.

When he finally caught his breath, he heard clanking noises behind him. He turned around. Through an open door, he saw the kitchen of a diner. His stomach began to growl with hunger as he sneaked inside.

It was perfect. The tables were full of old people, and they all looked rich to him—especially the man who had taken off his wristwatch to show his friend.

The kid grabbed the watch and ran. He was already out the door when a cry rang through the diner: *"Stop! Thief!"*

To go after him, turn to page 22.

The Kid panicked. The Welfare folks were onto him. He'd have to leave—for good. He hurried into Tracy's bedroom and stuffed the baseball into his pocket.

A thunderclap from outside made him jump. He hated to go out into the rain, but he had no choice. As he passed the dresser he spotted Tracy's wallet. He grabbed it, then pried open the window and climbed out.

Rain pelted the Kid as he stood in the alley and pulled out the cash from the wallet. As he went to toss the billfold into a trash can, he caught sight of Tracy's badge. He held it and looked up at the detective's apartment, blinking away the raindrops.

A door slammed, and three people came out of the building. The Kid's mouth fell open in shock. He saw two men, Flattop and Itchy, stuffing Tracy into the backseat of a car.

He jammed the wallet into his pocket as the car spun away from the curb. The Kid lunged, pulling himself onto the bumper with the trunk handle. As he held on tight the car skidded away at breakneck speed.

Where are they all going? Find out on page 34.

As Big Boy pulled Tess through the conference room, Numbers shouted, "There are a billion cops out there!"

"*Cops?*" Big Boy's jaw dropped. "OK, this is it. Lock the doors. Burn the records. Get your guns."

Numbers looked at Tess. "Gee, boss, you've taken Tracy's girl?"

"Someone set us up!" Big Boy snapped. "They're gonna get us for kidnapping!"

He pulled Tess down the stairs and through the main room of the club. Club members welcomed in the New Year by dancing to Breathless's singing. No one noticed Big Boy's henchmen locking doors and bolting windows.

Big Boy dragged Tess through a back door into the club's garage. Already two cars had lined up facing the garage door, and Flattop and Itchy were climbing into a third. As Big Boy pushed Tess into the backseat of a black sedan, Numbers jumped into the driver's seat and started it up.

"Now!" Big Boy yelled. "Hit your horn!"

The cars began moving toward the closed door, picking up speed. As Numbers stepped on the gas Big Boy reached for the door handle.

The car took off, but Big Boy rolled out of the car, pulling Tess onto the garage floor with him.

Where's Tracy when he's needed? Find out on page 16.

By the time Tracy returned to the opera house, the audience was leaving. As he caught up with Tess, reporters crowded around, firing questions at the veteran cop.

"Who pulled off the killings, Tracy?"

"Is it true you're moving up to chief of police?"

Tracy managed to shake the reporters without giving any answers. But Tess wanted to know the answer to the last question. It wasn't easy being in love with a cop. If Tracy was chief of police, he wouldn't be out on the streets so much—and she'd see him more often. When they were walking alone to their favorite diner, she asked, "Don't you want to take over Chief Brandon's job? The only reason he hasn't retired is because he's waiting for you to come to your senses."

Tracy shook his head. Being a cop was in his bones. He couldn't be anything else. "Nobody's going to put Big Boy Caprice behind bars sitting at a desk. And—"

Just then Tracy was hit in the stomach. A kid bounced off him and streaked down the street.

"He stole my watch!" shouted an old man from the door of the diner.

In a flash, Tracy was off and running.

The kid was fast, especially when he knew a cop was after him. As he crossed the tracks into the railroad yard, he just missed being hit by a train.

A Catch-a-Crook Adventure

The kid barged into a shack at the edge of the yard. Across the room a big, hideous man glared at him while eating a piece of fried chicken.

"You didn't save me no chicken, Steve?" the kid said.

Steve tossed him a bone. "Let's see the stuff."

When the kid slapped the watch down, Steve snarled in disgust. "That's all?"

The kid nodded, and Steve moved toward him. Using the back of his hand, Steve knocked the kid against the wall. He was about to do more when a shadow fell across the room.

"Hey, tough guy, try that on me!" Dick Tracy said from the doorway.

Steve reached for a wooden plank. Swinging wildly, he almost clipped Tracy in the head.

Tracy ducked. Steve may have been strong, but he wasn't as quick as Tracy. All it took was three punches to send Steve flying through the back wall of the shack.

As Tracy handcuffed the unconscious man he felt the kid's wide eyes staring at him. He'd have to do something with the little crook—but what?

To find out what Dick Tracy does with the boy, turn to page 29.
To discover the trouble that's brewing across town, turn to page 9.

"**I** hope you understand, Mr. Tracy," came Mrs. Skaff's voice from behind the closed door. "A single man can't just take in a child off the streets. He belongs in an orphanage. It's the law."

Tracy heard a commotion in his bedroom. When he went inside, his heart sank. The Kid was gone, and the window was open. Rain slapped onto Tracy's floor as thunder boomed outside.

"He has to be processed through the proper channels," Mrs. Skaff called through the door. "Then we'll place him in an orphanage."

Tracy went back to the door. "Mrs. Skaff," he said, yanking it open, "if you'll leave this to me—"

He came face-to-face with Flattop. Behind him stood Itchy, grinning evilly.

"We don't want no kid, copper," said Itchy, dropping the high-pitched female voice. Flattop lifted a tommy gun to Tracy's face.

There was nothing Tracy could do. Itchy and Flattop forced him downstairs, then outside and into a car. Together they sped off into the rainy night.

But they all missed one thing. Behind them, clutching onto the back of the car, was the Kid.

Where are they taking Tracy? Find out on page 34.

Tracy raced out of the club, past Chief Brandon's men, and ran toward the river.

He didn't stop until he reached the drawbridge. There, he hid in the shadows and kept his eyes glued to a large hole in the riverbank.

A sewer hole. That *had* to be what the foghorn echoed through.

Tracy bristled with anger as Big Boy emerged from the hole, pulling Tess. Big Boy dragged his hostage onto the bridge, and Tess fought him all the way. Beneath them, a cruise ship passed. Fireworks shot upward from the deck as people began shouting, "Happy New Year!"

Before Big Boy and Tess could get to the top, the drawbridge began to rise. Tracy ran toward them.

Big Boy had only one choice—the gear house at the bottom of the bridge. He yanked Tess into it.

Tracy sprinted to the gear house and pulled the door open. He stepped onto a platform surrounded by monstrous metal gears and levers. With teeth two feet thick, the gears moved slowly, groaning with the weight of the bridge.

"Hands up, copper!" came Big Boy's voice in the darkness. "We've got to talk. I did not kidnap this woman. Drop that gun or my next bullet's got her name on it!"

Tracy pivoted to his left, and his eyes widened with shock. Tess was tied to a moving gear, slowly rolling upward. Behind the gear was Big Boy, clutching his gun.

"Don't do it, Tracy!" Tess cried out.

Tracy threw down his gun. It dropped into the gears and fired by itself.

Big Boy spun around when he heard the stray bullet hit the wall behind him.

Immediately Tracy ducked behind some gears and crawled toward Big Boy.

"Tracy!" Big Boy called out. "Playing hide-and-seek, eh? Look, this is not fair. I was framed. I never kidnapped this girl. Tracy, where are you? Come out!" His eyes darted wildly. "I want to live and you want to live. I'll wait you out, Tracy! You think I don't know you're here?"

Tracy was inches from Big Boy now, still hidden. He grabbed a wrench and threw it against a back wall. When Big Boy spun around, Tracy sprang up and punched him in the jaw. Big Boy went sprawling across the floor.

Tracy quickly began to untie Tess. Behind him, Big Boy picked up a pipe and attacked. Tracy fell with a thud.

Tess looked on in horror as Big Boy hit Tracy again and again. Wriggling away, Tracy rose to his feet. With his last ounce of strength he pummeled Big Boy into the wall, then turned back to help Tess.

"I knew you'd find me, Tracy," Tess said, smiling. But her face went pale with fear when she saw Big Boy coming back for more.

Suddenly a shot rang out above them. Tracy looked up and saw a familiar figure in the doorway.

The faceless stranger—with a gun.

"Don't move, Big Boy. Get your hands up, Tracy," the stranger said. "I outsmarted you, Big Boy. I knew you'd panic. I brought you down with kidnapping, the only crime you didn't commit. Now I'm taking it all. With you two out of the way, I'll own this town."

Behind Tracy, Tess was inches away from being crushed by two gears. She struggled against the ropes as the faceless stranger pointed his gun at Tracy.

Out of the corner of his eye Tracy caught a movement in the doorway. Had any of Big Boy's men survived? he wondered.

Suddenly the Blank pitched forward. His gun went flying.

He had been tackled from behind—by the Kid!

Instantly Big Boy scrambled to his feet. He grabbed the gun and fired two shots at the stranger. Tracy swung at Big Boy, landing a roundhouse punch that sent him crumpling to the floor, unconscious.

But the danger wasn't over. Tess was still tied

to the gear as it rolled upward to meet the teeth of another gear. Her head was inches away from being crushed. "Tracy, hurry!" she screamed.

Tracy raced over and pulled her free. She threw her arms around him, and they stood in a tight embrace.

The Kid was at the other end of the room, trying not to blush.

When they finally let go, Tracy walked over to the motionless stranger. He was out cold. Tracy exhaled, then put his wrist-radio to his mouth. "Tracy to Chief Brandon," he said wearily. "I think you'd better come over to the gear house by the bridge. And, uh, happy New Year."

Another boat passed under the bridge, full of loud passengers. As they all sang happily and blew into noisemakers, Tracy, Tess, and the Kid stared into the distance.

The story isn't over till it's over. For a happy ending, turn to page 63.

Dick Tracy and Tess Trueheart watched patiently as the young watch thief stuffed himself at Mike's Diner.

"You got a name?" Tracy asked him.

"Kid," he replied, munching away.

"What's the name your mother and father gave you?" continued Tracy.

"What mother and father?"

Tracy exhaled. "Looks like I have to call the Welfare Department," he said to Tess.

The Kid bolted from his seat, but Tracy grabbed his collar. "Hey, where are you going?"

"You ain't sticking me in no orphanage!" the Kid protested. "I been there."

Sam's voice barked over Tracy's wrist-radio, *"Tracy! We need you at Southside Warehouse—now!"*

The Kid stared at the radio in awe.

"Take the Kid to my place," Tracy said to Tess. "I'll send the squad car." He slapped money on the table and raced out.

Tess sighed, then leaned over to get her purse. Out of the corner of her eye she could see the Kid reaching for Tracy's money. "Touch that money and I'll break your arm," she said.

The Kid glowered at her. "I don't like dames."

"Good," Tess replied. "Neither do I."

Tracy walked through the warehouse with Sam,

Pat, and Chief Brandon. They were too late. The place was empty—except for some walnut shells and one sapphire earring. Tracy pocketed the earring and lifted the shells with a handkerchief. "Sam, fingerprint these," he said. "Pat, bring in Flattop, Itchy, and Mumbles."

"What have they got to do with a handful of walnuts?" Chief Brandon asked.

"We've got to find Lips," Tracy said. "Fast."

It didn't take long for Sam to drag the crooks into the police station. In the police interrogation room someone was bound to reveal Lips's whereabouts.

Tracy began with Mumbles, questioning him into the wee hours of the morning. Mumbles squirmed under the hot lights. There was nothing in the room but a chair, a table, and a watercooler shaped like a polar bear.

Mumbles hated the heat. He hated the polar bear. His throat was dry from thirst.

"Where is Lips Manlis?" Tracy asked for what seemed like the hundredth time.

Mumbles mumbled, "Idonnonuthn."

Tracy took a swig from a tumbler filled with water. "Where is Lips Manlis?" he repeated.

"Gttahvsmwtryucntdthstome."

"Got to have some water, Mumbles?" Tracy

asked. He lifted the tumbler and drank the whole thing down.

That did it. Mumbles screamed, "Alrightalright—BigBoydidithekildLpsMnlisBigBoydidithekildLps…"

"OK, Mumbles, that's your testimony," Tracy said. He pulled Mumbles out of his chair. "Get him out of here," Tracy ordered an officer.

Sam turned to Tracy. "You forced him to confess, Tracy," he said, "even if you didn't understand it."

Sam was right—but that didn't stop Tracy. He rounded up the other two thugs and brought them to the Club Ritz with Pat and Sam.

At the club, Big Boy was running a rehearsal for the stage show. Breathless Mahoney, the singer, was slumped on the piano, half-asleep. The chorus girls were practically falling over. Even 88 Keys, the best piano player in town, was dragging. They all stopped when Tracy barged in.

"Hello, Big Boy," Tracy said, pushing the three gangsters toward their boss. "Brought your garbage."

Big Boy took a walnut from his pocket and cracked it. "This is a private club, copper."

"The place belongs to Lips, Big Boy. Not you."

"Wrong, copper. I made a deal with Lips today."

"Where is he?"

"I think he left town or something."

Breathless came into view behind Big Boy. Tracy noticed she wore only one earring—a sapphire, like the one in his pocket.

"You know," Tracy said, looking at the walnut in Big Boy's hand, "walnuts must be bad for the brain. You're sloppy, Big Boy—and you're under arrest for the murders of five mobsters at the Seventh Street Garage."

As the cops led Big Boy away Flattop called out, "See you in a half-hour, boss."

Big Boy looked over his shoulder at the performers. "This ain't a break!" he yelled. "Keep rehearsing!"

Now that Big Boy was out of the way, Tracy had to find out about the earring. As Sam and Pat took Big Boy to the station, Tracy went back into the club. Breathless had gone to her dressing room, and he quickly tracked her down.

She tried not to look surprised when Tracy entered. "What are you up to, honey?" she said. "Are you going to arrest me?"

"No," Tracy replied. "I want you to tell me who killed Lips Manlis, in court."

Breathless just laughed. She moved toward Tracy, looking deeply into his eyes.

Tracy wasn't going to fall for her. He turned to leave. "Look, Big Boy's in jail. You're the one who can keep him there. Give me a call."

Is Big Boy caught for good? Find out on page 39.

Lips Manlis meets his doom when Big Boy Caprice's men give him a cement bath.

After taking over the Club Ritz, Big Boy greedily counts the money that comes with it as Mumbles looks on.

The Kid stuffs himself at Mike's Diner after being rescued from the streets by Detective Dick Tracy.

Breathless Mahoney really knows how to entertain the crowd at the Club Ritz's opening night.

The Kid saves Dick Tracy's life by helping him escape from the basement moments before the furnace explodes.

Dick Tracy gives the Kid a detective's badge after the Kid saves his life.

To frame Dick Tracy, the mysterious faceless stranger steals samples of the detective's handwriting.

Flattop convinces Tess Trueheart to follow Big Boy into the Club Ritz's secret tunnel.

88 Keys squinted as he walked into the dark streetcar barn. A table, a small suitcase, and an envelope were all he could see.

He was scared. A stranger had phoned him and ordered him to come to this address. Just a voice—a weird voice.

Suddenly someone croaked through a microphone, "Open the suitcase." 88 Keys jumped. It was the same voice that had called him, strangled-sounding, like someone talking through a closed mouth.

A person moved into the dim light. He wore a trench coat and carried a microphone. 88 Keys tried to make out his features, but they were covered by the shadow of a wide-brimmed hat.

The piano player quickly opened the suitcase. He gasped. It was packed with money.

"Your first payment," the stranger said, using the microphone again. "All you have to do is hand the envelope to Big Boy. You don't know where it came from, and you never saw me." The stranger lifted his head into the light.

88 Keys thought he would faint. Under the hat was nothing but a lump of flesh—no eyes, no nose, no mouth. He felt himself start to shake.

The light flicked off, and the stranger was gone.

To find out what the letter says, turn to page 37.

Screeeeeeee! Flattop slammed on the brakes in front of Tess's apartment building. Once inside, the men shoved Tracy down to the basement.

Big Boy and Numbers were waiting. As Flattop pushed Tracy onto a chair next to the furnace, Big Boy came closer. "Tracy," he said, "we thought you'd be more comfortable here while your girlfriend's away at work. Now, my associates, here, would very much like to see you have an accident. But I say no—I want you on *my* side. Think about it, Tracy. Your gal deserves something better than this dump. You could treat her like a princess with this." He removed a roll of money from Numbers's briefcase. "It's yours, Tracy."

All eyes were on Tracy, including the Kid's. He held his breath as he stared through the basement window. Tracy wouldn't take a bribe, would he? the Kid wondered.

Big Boy smiled as Tracy picked up the money. "This is a lot of dough, Big Boy...and you are guilty of attempting to bribe an officer of the law!"

Tracy threw the money at Big Boy's face. The detective whirled toward Flattop and Itchy, but he was outnumbered. They wrestled him back into the chair and tied him down. Itchy picked up a wrench off the floor, then approached the furnace.

"You insult me, you stupid cop," Big Boy snarled. "I offer you the keys to a kingdom and you tell me you're an officer of the law. *I am the law. Me!*" He turned toward the stairs. "Boys, you guaranteed it would look like an accident. Don't disappoint me."

As Big Boy and Numbers went upstairs Itchy raised the wrench. He held it high for a few seconds, then slammed it down. The safety valve smashed off and steam billowed out. With a burst of laughter, Flattop and Itchy ran up the stairs.

Tracy's eyes darted desperately around the room. They stopped when they got to the window. "Kid!" he shouted. "Get away! The place is going to blow!"

The Kid fumbled for his pocket. He pulled out the baseball and hurled it through the window.

Broken glass showered into the basement. The Kid climbed in and jumped to the floor. The furnace shook violently, and steam spewed into the room. The Kid grabbed a piece of broken glass. He knelt behind Tracy and began to cut the rope.

Suddenly the rope split. Tracy pulled his hands apart and leapt out of the chair. Drenched with sweat, he glanced at the furnace. It was bursting at the seams. The truth hit him like a sledgehammer.

They were goners.

Is this it for Tracy and the Kid? Find out on page 5.

The smell of homemade muffins made Tess smile. It was wonderful to be back at her mother's house. She felt so relaxed—until she thought of Tracy. Then she slumped back into the kitchen chair.

Mrs. Trueheart took the muffins out of the oven. "Tracy will *never* take the chief of police job," she said. "He has to be in the line of fire. It takes a lot of understanding to love a man like that."

Suddenly Tess had a feeling that she should be with Tracy. This was no time to leave him alone. She stood up. "Can I put some muffins in a bag, Mother?" she asked. "I'm going back tonight."

Instead of going home, Tess went to the place where she worked, a greenhouse in the middle of the City. She had a plan: She'd send Tracy some flowers and invite him to have a talk with her.

She began to arrange a bouquet of lilies. When she turned to wrap up the flowers, she froze.

Someone was waiting for her—a mysterious figure holding a knife, a person whose face was a featureless lump. Tess dropped the flowers.

"I'm working for Big Boy," the intruder said in a weird voice. "He wants you."

To find out what else the stranger is up to, turn to page 61.

That night, in the Club Ritz conference room, Big Boy was silent as 88 Keys read him a note. The note had been given to the piano player by a man with no face—the Blank—in a secret meeting.

As 88 Keys read the note Breathless looked on curiously.

"'If you kill Dick Tracy, you will be the prime suspect, and the City will mobilize against you. But for ten percent of your business, we guarantee Tracy will not be a problem for you anymore....'" 88 Keys lifted his eyes from the note. "What can you lose, Big Boy? If they don't deliver, you don't pay."

Big Boy's face twisted into a look of utter disgust. "You're a piano player. What do you want to be, a radish? Don't bring me a deal from someone you never saw and don't know how to contact." He turned to Numbers. "Get him out of here," he said. "Make him go play the piano."

Later, Big Boy bustled downstairs and into the club. His scowl turned into a smile. Opening night looked like a success. The gambling tables were full, and Breathless was singing her heart out.

Big Boy finally had what he wanted. The entire crime world was there, eating out of his hands.

REEEEEEOOOOOO!

He cringed at the sound of his cop alarm.

"Take it easy," Big Boy announced when the

club flew into a panic. "Everything's OK."

He walked to a control panel. With a flick of a switch the gambling tables revolved into the walls and were replaced by dining tables. In an instant the Club Ritz became a fashionable restaurant.

The front door burst open. Tracy stormed inside with an army of cops. He surveyed the familiar faces—Johnny Ramm, Texie Garcia, Ribs Mocca. "The gang's all here," Tracy said. "Looks like a class reunion." He threw an envelope onto a table. "Here's my invitation—a search warrant."

Off to one side he caught a glimpse of Breathless. As she continued singing a slow love ballad she stared at him and smiled. Tracy felt a lump form in his throat.

Unseen by all but Tracy, a gray-haired waiter slipped up the back steps.

Just then an eager young cop ran up to Tracy. "There's no gambling here," the cop said with a shrug. "No nothing."

Tracy looked around. Men and women chatted at tables. Waiters scurried about, taking orders.

Big Boy and Pruneface just smiled.

Was Tracy fooled? Find out on page 11.
To discover who the gray-haired waiter is and what he's up to, turn to page 60.

By the next day, Tracy had results—but not the ones he was looking for: no fingerprints on the walnut shells, headlines about police brutality against Big Boy, and an order to report to D.A. Fletcher's office with Chief Brandon.

When Tracy and Brandon got there, Fletcher was angry. "How can I support a police detective who keeps making false arrests of private citizens and throwing them in jail?" he bellowed.

Tracy squirmed as Sam's voice blared over his wrist-radio. *"Tracy, Tess is waiting for you with the Kid at Marshall and Bradbury's department store—the boys' department..."*

"Chief," Fletcher said to Brandon, "I am a candidate for mayor. If you can't control Detective Tracy, you'll have to take him off duty—or I'll prosecute him and take *you* off duty."

With that, Fletcher stormed out.

When Tracy got to the store, Tess was waiting for the Kid to try on a suit she had picked out. She looked toward the dressing room and sighed. "Sam says we have to take him to the orphanage tomorrow afternoon."

"Where's he going to stay tonight?" Tracy asked.

Before Tess could answer, a clerk rushed in, frantic. "The boy ran out the back door!"

Tracy took off. He found the Kid halfway down the block, pulling his old clothes on over his underwear. "Come here," he said. "What's the matter with you?"

The Kid spun around. "I ain't wearing no suit. A suit's for school, and that means the orphanage."

"Look," Tracy said, "if you don't want to wear a suit, then go back in and tell her. Are you going to run away every time somebody says something you don't like?"

The remark hit home. The Kid thought about it, then walked back toward the store. Tracy joined him.

Neither of them noticed Flattop and Itchy watching from a parked car across the street.

The rest of the day went smoothly. After the Kid picked out clothes for himself, Tracy took him and Tess to lunch at the diner, and then they all went for a drive in the country. When Tracy pulled up to Tess's apartment that night, the Kid was asleep on her lap.

"Nice day," Tess remarked, smiling.

"Yeah," Tracy said. He felt awkward. For so long, Tess had been the one who always wanted to talk about their future together. Today *he* felt like trying. "I've been thinking...about you living alone."

"I *like* living alone," Tess said. "You know that. I'm not the lonely type."

"Well...that's something we have in common."

"Yeah..." Tess said with a nod. "We have that in common."

Tracy took a deep breath. "Well, don't you think that since we have so much in common it might be...a good idea if we just...went ahead and..."

"Yes?" Tess said, her eyes bright with anticipation. Could this be? Was Tracy going to propose?

The Kid began to stir. Tracy hopped out of the car and went around to the passenger side. After helping Tess out, he left the Kid inside the car and walked Tess to her building. "Look," he said, "what I'm trying to say is—"

Suddenly he heard the Kid scream, *"Hey! Tracy, watch out!"*

Tracy whirled around. There was a car moving down the street. Its lights were off, but something gleamed in the passenger window—a tommy gun.

"Merry Christmas, copper!" a voice shouted as the night exploded with the sound of gunfire.

Quick! Turn to page 14.

At the Midway Hotel a figure in a trench coat and hat burst through the front door and dashed up the stairs.

The night clerk looked up and sneered. "Close the door!" he shouted in vain. Grumbling, he hobbled to the door himself.

Moments later he heard muffled shouting from above. "You can't blackmail me, Dick Tracy! Put that gun away! I don't have to pay you!"

The clerk quietly reached for the phone and dialed the police.

In room four twenty-nine, 88 Keys stopped imitating D.A. Fletcher's voice and propped Dick Tracy up in a chair. The piano player had fulfilled his part of the bargain.

Across the room the faceless stranger examined Fletcher's body on the floor. His silencer gun had done the trick; Fletcher was dead.

The stranger then placed his gun in Tracy's hand. After signaling for 88 Keys to climb out the window, the faceless man passed a bottle of ammonia under Tracy's nose. Then he slipped out of the room.

When the authorities arrived moments later, they found Tracy with a gun in his hand. The dazed detective was hovering over the body of D.A. Fletcher. Everyone knew the two men hadn't been getting along, but no one had expected *this*.

*   *   *

Big Boy was happy to give a ten-percent payment to 88 Keys. "I gotta hand it to you, 88," he said jubilantly. "Your people got Tracy out of the way." He turned to the other gangsters in the Club Ritz conference room. "Boys, we're back in business!"

That evening the Kid was allowed to leave the orphanage to visit Tracy in jail. The Kid was escorted by Chief Brandon. Neither of them knew what to say. The evidence was stacked against Tracy, but they couldn't actually *believe* it.

Tracy didn't want to talk about it. He was more concerned about Tess. "Why would somebody kidnap Tess and not even ask for ransom?" he wondered aloud, pacing the floor. "I could find her in eight hours if I could just get back on the street."

A guard looked into the cell. Brandon saw him and stood up. "They should be coming to transfer you to County Jail in a little while, Tracy."

As Brandon walked out the Kid turned to Tracy. "It doesn't matter, does it, Tracy?" he said. "When you're honest and people still don't believe you, it just doesn't matter...."

Tracy looked the Kid in the eye. "It matters if some people do."

The Kid looked away. For a moment neither of them knew what to say. Then the Kid reached into his pocket, saying, "I got my permanent certificate."

"Oh? I thought you had to pick a name."

"I did." He pulled out the certificate. On it were printed the words *Dick Tracy, Jr.*

Speechless, Tracy stared at the certificate.

"I believe in you, Tracy," the Kid said firmly.

When the guards came for Tracy, he trudged glumly to a waiting squad car. He sat in the backseat and looked at the driver and his partner.

He did a double take when he saw Pat and Sam.

Tracy was stunned. "What are you two doing here?"

Sam leaned over to unlock Tracy's handcuffs. "It's a long trip to County Jail. I'd say it would take us at least eight hours to get there."

Tracy smiled. It was nice having friends in the right places. He flexed his freed hands and began barking orders. "Call headquarters. Get a car to meet us at Thirty-eighth and Central—and tell the boys to bring the polar bear watercooler from the interrogation room...."

As the car sped through town Tracy sat back and thought through his plan. He didn't know if it would work, but one thing was certain: Big Boy hadn't seen the last of him yet.

To discover Tracy's plan, turn to page 47.

In the conference room, Pruneface and Influence looked up at Big Boy. Influence opened his mouth to ask a question, but Big Boy held up a hand to silence him.

Big Boy stepped down from the table and looked toward the door. He could sneak upstairs and surprise the cop, no sweat. But he had a better idea....

After sitting down at the conference table, he picked up the telephone and dialed a phony number. He kept his finger on the receiver hook to make sure that the call didn't really go through.

"Okay, Freddy," he said, making up a name, "get down to the Southside Warehouse. Big payoff."

Influence and Pruneface both smiled. They knew that the eavesdropper upstairs was listening to every word—and would pass the message along to Tracy.

"Boys," said Big Boy under his breath, "let's get him."

The three men grabbed their guns and ran upstairs.

Where's Tracy when Bug needs him? Find out on page 55.

Tracy drove behind Breathless's car, staying far enough away so she wouldn't see him. Her car stopped in front of the Club Ritz. Tracy parked close enough to watch as she got out of the car and went inside the club. Two men walked in after her. Tracy recognized them—Influence and Pruneface, two of the City's biggest gangsters.

As they walked into the club Tracy noticed that only the second floor was lit up. He grabbed a pair of binoculars from his glove compartment and ran into the building across from the club. He climbed to the second floor, found a window, and peered out, focusing his binoculars carefully.

Tracy's eyes widened. He put his wrist-radio to his mouth. "Pat, Sam, come in!" he said. "It looks like we've got every top hood in town in one room at the Club Ritz: Big Boy, Flattop, Itchy, Pruneface, Ribs Mocca, Johnny Ramm, Texie Garcia, Spud Spaldoni..."

"What are they doing together?" came Pat's voice from the wrist-radio. *"Most of those guys hate each other!"*

"I intend to find out. Get over here fast!"

At police headquarters Pat and Sam rushed for the door.

What's going on in the club? The answer's on page 51.

The car sped to Thirty-eighth and Central—Mumbles's apartment building. The other car arrived seconds later.

Mumbles was in his room. As soon as the thug opened the door, Tracy slammed him up against a wall. "Talk, you cockroach!" he shouted. "Who set me up?"

"Idntsetyouupwhatyamean?" said Mumbles.

Tracy grabbed the polar bear watercooler and shoved it in Mumbles's face. Yanking off the top of the bear's head, he exposed a wire recorder inside. "Don't want to talk? Maybe I'll play this for Big Boy."

He flipped a switch inside the bear, and they heard Mumbles's voice say, *"BgBokldLpsMnls."*

Mumbles didn't seem to care. He mumbled, "WhdIcrwhtyoudo?"

Tracy rewound the tape and played it again. This time he held his fingers around the wire, slowing the recording down. The voice was deep and clear:

"Big...Boy...killed...Lips...Manlis."

Flicking the recorder off, Tracy called out, "Come on, boys, let's go play this for Big Boy!"

"Wait!" Suddenly Mumbles's voice was as clear as a radio announcer's. "88 Keys set you up. Big Boy paid him to get you out of the way!"

"88 Keys and Big Boy, huh?" Tracy said. "OK, boys, take him away."

* * *

Chief Brandon was about to take the Kid back to the orphanage when he got a call. The voice on the other end was crackly and distorted—and sinister. "You interested in getting Big Boy?" it said.

"Who is this?" Brandon demanded.

"Go to Thirty-eighth and Grand and wait for a call." At that, the line went dead.

Thirty-eighth and Grand. That was the Club Ritz. Brandon hung up the phone and turned to his men. "Watch the Kid till I get back."

Halfway across town, Sam drove his squad car away from Mumbles's building. "So what do we do?" Sam called over his shoulder. "Grab 88 Keys or go straight for Big Boy?"

Tracy furrowed his brow, deep in thought. "Is the enemy of my enemy my friend? Or is the enemy of my friend my enemy...? Or is the enemy of my enemy my enemy?"

"What did he say?" Pat asked Sam.

Tracy nodded. "The enemy of my enemy is my enemy!" He sat bolt upright. "The Club Ritz, and step on it!"

In the crowded main room of the club Big Boy grabbed the ringing phone. "Caprice speaking."

A Catch-a-Crook Adventure

"Better take a look in your attic," said a muffled, electronic-sounding voice. "Something's fishy."

"Who is this?" Big Boy demanded. He heard only a click.

Meanwhile, Tracy and Pat were running across the neighboring rooftops toward the club. "Tracy, why are we going to the roof?" Pat asked.

"Pat," Tracy replied, "whoever framed me is framing Big Boy."

"On the roof?"

Brandon pulled to the curb across the street from the Club Ritz. Around him, half a dozen other squad cars parked. He turned off his engine and wondered what to do next. *Wait for a call*, the anonymous caller had told him.

"Come in, Chief Brandon!" said the dispatcher's voice over the radio.

"Brandon here," he shot back.

"You got a call here, sir...a strange one."

"It better be something about the Club Ritz. I'm here with a dozen men and no reason to break in."

"Well, sir, it looks like you have a reason now...."

Brandon listened as the cop told him about the new message the strange caller had left for him.

Behind Brandon, unseen by anyone, the Kid hopped off the trunk of the car. Keeping to the shadows, he scampered toward the club.

* * *

At that moment Tracy and Pat jumped onto the Club Ritz rooftop. They peered through the skylight into the attic. What they saw made Tracy's jaw drop open. Tess was gagged and tied to a chair.

"Jumping Jiminy," Pat said.

Crrrrrack! A bullet smashed through the skylight. Tracy and Pat hit the deck.

Flattop had fired the gun. He and Big Boy had burst into the attic and seen the cops through the skylight. They had also seen Tess. "What's she doing here?" Big Boy screamed. "We've been framed for kidnapping!"

Flattop untied Tess. She struggled as he and Big Boy dragged her toward a heavy steel door.

Taking careful aim, Flattop fired at Tracy through the skylight, then headed for the door.

With an explosion of shattering glass Tracy crashed into the attic. As Tracy hit the floor Flattop pulled Tess through the door and locked it.

Outside, Tess screamed for help. Flattop's reply sent a chill up Tracy's spine: "You're coming with me, sweet pea. Anybody shoots at me, I shoot you!"

***Where is Big Boy taking Tess? Find out on page 21.
Is it all over for Tracy? Find out on page 16.***

Tonight was Big Boy's night. Every face was turned his way in the second-floor conference room of the Club Ritz. All the gangsters who had once hated him were now listening quietly.

"You guys have pulled a lot on me, but I forgive you," Big Boy announced. "The past is the past. A boss must always look to the future—and the future is *me*."

The gangsters began to protest, but Big Boy pounded his fist on the table. "We're all split up now. It's easy for the cops to control us. So we form a company, see? Each of us is on the board of directors, and I'm the chairman of the board."

"Why you?" Spud Spaldoni asked.

"'Cause I have a vision," Big Boy replied. "A big boss must always have a vision. I say we move in on the small stores and businesses in this town. Every time some citizen buys a hamburger, we get a nickel. Every time a guy gets a haircut, we get a dime. Together we will own this town!"

"But why you?" Spaldoni repeated, louder.

Big Boy gave Itchy a signal that no one else saw. Immediately Itchy left the room.

"When do we kill Tracy?" Influence thundered.

"If anything happens to Tracy, they put the finger on me," Big Boy replied. "You leave Tracy to me."

"I say we rub him out now!" Pruneface retorted.

Big Boy leaned forward. "*I say:* Get behind me and we all profit. Challenge me and we all go down! There was one Napoleon, one Washington, one *me!*"

Spud Spaldoni stood up. "I'm out," he muttered. "I got a good business. I'll take my chances alone." He and his bodyguard went to the door.

Flattop stood up to block Spaldoni's path.

"Let him go," Big Boy said. "It's still a free country."

The room fell silent as everyone watched Spaldoni leave. Big Boy's eyes narrowed. "Maybe he'll have a change of heart," he said.

Soon after Pat and Sam parked across from the Club Ritz, Itchy walked out the front door. He quietly placed a small paper bag inside a limousine at the curb, then went back into the club.

Suddenly Sam spotted someone crouched on the second-floor ledge. He did a double take. "Tracy!" he said into his wrist-radio. "What are you doing up there?"

"Bring the car under the streetlight," Tracy's voice answered. *"I can't hear a thing up here."*

Sam reached for the ignition, but when the club's door smacked open, he and Pat ducked to the floor. They carefully looked up to see Spud

Spaldoni and his henchman get into the limo.

BA-ROOOOOM!

The police car rocked back and forth as Spaldoni's limo exploded into a million pieces.

"Tracy!" Sam yelled. Scrambling back up into the front seat, he and Pat looked up at the ledge.

Tracy was still there, shell-shocked after seeing the explosion. Sam revved the car and headed for the club.

As he pulled up in front Tracy slid down a light pole and hopped onto the top of Sam's car. Sam floored the gas pedal and sped into the night.

In the Club Ritz conference room the gangsters gawked out the window at the shattered limo.

Big Boy shook his head. "Very upsetting," he said. "Very upsetting."

"All right, Big Boy," Pruneface said, "we'll leave Tracy to you. When does the board meet?"

"Tomorrow night, downstairs," Big Boy said with a grin. "The reopening of the Club Ritz, and you're all invited. I pick up the tab."

In Big Boy's mind it was all very simple now. The other gangsters were too scared to protest. The City was his.

What he didn't count on was the stranger lurking across the street—the mysterious figure with a long coat, a wide hat, and no face.

*   *   *

When Tracy heard a knock at the door the next morning, he was in his bathroom, brushing his teeth. As he went to answer it the Kid followed him, tossing a baseball in the air. He smiled. It was good to see the little guy looking normal for a change.

"Who is it?" Tracy called out.

"Mr. Tracy," a voice answered, "I'm Mrs. Skaff, from the Welfare Department. I'm afraid we're going to have to take the boy to the orphanage."

Tracy felt his heart skip. At first he had wanted to get rid of the Kid, but now he wanted to protect him. He finished getting dressed in the living room. "Just give me one minute, Mrs. Skaff," he said.

Behind him, the Kid backed into Tracy's bedroom, slowly, quietly...

To follow the Kid, turn to page 20.
To find out what Tracy does, turn to page 24.

After a night chasing down Big Boy's men, Tracy was starving. He gobbled down a bowl of chili at Mike's Diner while the Kid slept in a booth behind him.

Tess stared at the floor, trying to think of the right words to say. She finally took a deep breath and said, "Tracy, I'm leaving."

Tracy stopped eating.

"I used to be afraid that maybe you'd never take some time and settle down," Tess said. She sighed sadly. "Now I know it."

Tracy looked at her, speechless.

"Good luck, Tracy," Tess said. "I'm sorry."

"Calling Dick Tracy!" Bug's voice shouted over the wrist-radio. *"Go to the Southside Warehouse!"*

Tracy ignored the message and continued staring at Tess.

"You've got Big Boy on the run now. That's good," Tess said.

"Calling Dick Tracy! Go to the Southside Warehouse!" Bug repeated.

Tess looked away. "Go ahead, Tracy. It's OK."

Standing up slowly, Tracy said, "I'll be back, Tess." He hesitated, then hurried out the door.

As soon as Tracy arrived at the warehouse, he knew he'd been tricked. He saw that Influence and Pruneface had tied up Bug in a large wooden crate. They were giving him a cement bath.

There was no time to lose. Tracy took off his coat and hat and propped them up to distract the gunmen. Then he ran to Bug.

Cement splattered onto both of them as Tracy untied Bug. Quickly they climbed out of the crate.

Pruneface swung around at the sight of the two men. He aimed his gun at Tracy.

Crrrack! A shot echoed through the warehouse.

Tracy turned to see Pruneface collapse to the floor. The gangster's eyes were wide with shock—and so were Tracy's when he saw who had fired the shot.

The gunman was a stranger with a trench coat and a wide-brimmed hat—and absolutely no features on his face.

Panicked, Influence ran for the door.

Big Boy exploded when Influence told him what had happened. "A guy with no face? How long's this guy been working for Tracy?"

Influence, Flattop, and Numbers looked at each other nervously. Only Breathless seemed relaxed.

Big Boy sprang up from his seat. "All right, I want this no-face dead, and I want Tracy dead!"

"But, Big Boy," Numbers said, "you wanted it to look like an accident!"

Big Boy fell silent. Flattop and Numbers exchanged an uneasy glance.

A Catch-a-Crook Adventure

A slow smile crept across Big Boy's face. "Yeah..." There *was* a way to deal with Tracy.

He turned to Numbers. "Get my car."

Numbers flew downstairs and ordered 88 Keys to come with them. As Numbers drove them around town Big Boy agreed to the faceless man's deal: ten percent of Big Boy's business if the stranger took care of Tracy.

Later that evening, as Tracy and the Kid sat in the diner, neither said a word. If they knew where Tess had gone, they could have gone after her. All she had told Brandon was that she was leaving town.

When Tracy and the Kid walked home, Tracy began to think about taking the chief of police job.

The Club Ritz was due to open in an hour. As 88 Keys rehearsed a new tune on the piano, he saw the headline of Breathless's newspaper:

TRACY SAVED BY FACELESS AIDE

88 Keys smiled. "He ain't going to *aid* Tracy," he said slyly. "He's going to *get* Tracy."

"How do you know?" Breathless asked.

"I know."

Breathless went to a telephone as 88 Keys played on. She quickly dialed Tracy's number.

Tracy answered the phone. He agreed to meet Breathless by the harbor. Within minutes they were standing at an empty dock. The City skyline loomed in the distance.

"I hear things I'm not supposed to hear," she said. "The man with no face—the Blank—is out to get you."

Tracy stopped walking. "Breathless," he said, "will you testify against Big Boy? If not, this is the last time we're going to meet."

"Why?" Breathless pleaded.

Tracy turned toward the water. When he looked back at her, he told her something he'd never imagined himself saying. "I'm in love with someone else."

Breathless left silently, choking back tears.

Tracy stayed for a moment, gazing sadly at the skyline. Then he headed straight for his office.

Later that night, the faceless stranger moved through Tracy's dark apartment with a small flashlight. When he found Tracy's desk, he took out a canceled check and an old grocery list.

Quietly he stuffed them into his pocket and left.

To find out what the mysterious stranger is up to, turn to page 61.
To find out where Tess has gone, turn to page 36.

On a flat cart, Big Boy and Tess rolled through the sewer tunnel that led from the club's wine room to the waterfront.

"Mr. Caprice," Tess yelled as they bounced over the joints in the tunnel, "I can assure you that taking me as a hostage will in no way keep Detective Tracy from his public duty."

"This is so awkward" was Big Boy's only reply.

"And he will have my complete support!" Tess continued.

"What a terrible way to usher in the New Year!" Big Boy moaned. They picked up speed, heading for an opening at the end. In a nervous, hysterical voice Big Boy cried, "I love a good ride. Don't you?"

The tunnel leveled off near the opening. Big Boy dragged his foot along the ground and brought the cart to a stop. He pulled Tess onto a deserted riverbank. Just to their left was a drawbridge that spanned the river.

"Oh, you louse!" Tess exclaimed.

Big Boy pulled her onto the bridge. "Believe me, this is not the way I wanted it to be."

Is Tess doomed? Find out on page 25.

The waiter raced to the second-floor conference room and looked up. The ceiling light shone on Pat's gray wig. His waiter disguise had worked so far. He hoped it would help him complete his mission.

In the attic above him, two men slid through the grimy skylight on a rope. One of them was Sam. The other was the police department's wire-tapping expert, Bug Bailey, who carried a backpack loaded with electronic equipment.

Quickly they dropped to the floor and pulled a drill out of Bug's backpack. They drilled a hole in the floor and immediately passed a wire through it.

Below them, Pat cleaned up the sawdust that had fallen through the hole. The wire emerged directly above the conference room light. Pat hopped onto a table and pulled a small microphone out of his pocket. He attached it to the wire, then nestled it in the light fixture.

As Bug and Sam hooked up the wire to a listening device, Pat ran out of the conference room and headed downstairs.

To join Tracy, turn to page 11.

88 Keys was thrilled. The faceless man had paid him to do another job, an easy one.

His first stop was a printing shop. He gave the shop owner the grocery list and canceled check that the faceless man had stolen from Tracy's apartment.

"Can you do it?" 88 Keys asked.

The owner looked as if he had been insulted. "I can copy *anyone's* handwriting."

"All right. In Tracy's handwriting, write this: 'I have evidence that will destroy you. Bring ten thousand dollars to room four twenty-nine, Midway Hotel.'"

In minutes 88 Keys was on his way to D.A. Fletcher's office to slip the note under the door.

That night Tracy sat at his desk, looking at police sketches of the faceless stranger. He had bad news for the Kid, and he didn't know how to break it to him.

Across the room the Kid sat staring at him, waiting. Brandon watched silently, his head bowed. Finally Tracy said, "The Welfare Department called. They're coming to take you to the orphanage tonight."

The Kid's eyes were like a wounded animal's. "What?" he said.

"Look," Tracy said, "I can't keep you with me.

I can't do it, Kid. It's against the law."

"Flowers, Tracy," Sam interrupted, putting a long box and a note on the detective's desk.

Tracy opened the note and read to himself, *Dear Dick, we really should talk this out. Please come to the greenhouse. Tess.*

Tracy frowned. "Chief," he said softly to Brandon, "would you take care of the Kid for a while?"

As Tracy dashed out the door, he passed the Welfare worker coming in.

The greenhouse was empty. Suspicious, Tracy walked around, looking for Tess. In a corner of the room, he spotted a bag of muffins spilled on the floor.

Suddenly the lights went out, and Tracy began to feel weak. His knees buckled.

"Relax, Tracy," came a distorted, filtered voice. "It won't kill you. It won't even hurt."

Tracy collapsed to the floor. As he struggled to open his eyes he couldn't help but notice the *hisssss* of poison gas shooting out from beneath the lilies.

"Just relax and go to sleep," the voice continued. "Your big career is over."

To discover what's in store for Tracy, turn to page 42.

Early that morning at Mike's Diner no one could stop the Kid from talking.

"...so that's when 88 Keys confessed that he and the Blank were in it together. The piano player told us that the faceless guy killed Fletcher!"

Tess nodded, holding back a smile. "Not bad."

"You know," Tracy said, "you're probably too smart to need this, but I think I'm going to give it to you anyway."

The Kid's eyes widened as Tracy pulled a small box out of his pocket. And the boy practically exploded with glee when he found a miniature wrist-radio inside. "Gee, Tracy," he said with a gasp. "Wow..."

Tracy and Tess shared a smile. Then Tracy leaned forward. "I've been thinking, Tess..."

"Yeah? What about?"

"Well...you living alone."

"I like living alone," Tess said, without much conviction. "We have that in common, I guess."

"Well..." Tracy cleared his throat. "When two people have a lot in common, they ought to do something about it."

He suddenly noticed that two small eyes were staring at him. "Uh-oh," the Kid said.

"Yes?" Tess asked Tracy, ignoring the Kid.

"Don't you think we'd be happier if we just..."

"What?"

Tracy fidgeted and shrugged. "What do you think?"

Tess looked him straight in the eye. "Dick Tracy, are you asking me to—"

"*Calling Dick Tracy!*" Pat's voice barked over the wrist-radio. "*Calling Dick Tracy! Robbery in progress. Metropolitan Bank.*"

"Hot diggety dog!" the Kid squealed, running for the door. He bolted outside and hopped into Tracy's car.

The detective's instincts pulled him out of his seat. He forced himself back.

"Well, what are you waiting for?" Tess asked. "A nice, safe desk?"

Tracy beamed. "Tess, you're one in a million."

Taking another small box from his pocket, he tossed it to Tess and left to join the Kid.

Tess opened it. The diamond ring inside glittered in the dull overhead lights of the diner.

A huge grin spread across Tess's face as Tracy's car roared away from the curb with Tracy and the Kid inside.

The End